R
M
(L.

ndon)

JEAN-PIERRE DE VILLIERS

ISBN: 9781796964400

Contents

JEAN-PIERRE DE VILLIERS

HOW
TO
OWN
YOUR
LIFE

Get out of your own way and
live your life with no regrets.

FIRST EDITION

JEAN-PIERRE DE VILLIERS

I would like to dedicate this book to my wife, Julia. It takes an extraordinary woman to be able to put up with me and stand by my side. I'm driven by my mission and obsessed about creating a brand that stands for something I believe in, inspiring the world and creating great leaders and role models. This is no easy task and most of the time means my wife, my best friend, takes second place. I'll never assume that this is easy to do, and I'm sure it takes a lot of understanding and patience! Thank you for always having my back Jules...

I love you.
JP

Foreword Lisa Nichols

Make Your Life a Bestselling Story.

JEAN-PIERRE DE VILLIERS

JP is the embodiment of love. Everything he does, every intention he sets, every strategy he develops, is all to bring out the best in each one of us. Through love and connection, JP has the ability to help you tap into the best version of yourself.

In this book 'How to Own Your Life' JP masterfully walks us through the ways we can learn how to dance with failure and make failure our friend. JP teaches us how to stand on our story, and not in our story. JP also teaches us how to set standards and get moving in such a way that our trajectory becomes absolutely unstoppable on our path to success. In whatever way, we define success for ourselves. JP is one of the leading coaches in the world, he has the ability to not only show us linear strategic moves, but also ways to make life better, stronger, and more exciting. JP does this with such love and such passion and understanding that just his mere words, helps us dismiss our limiting beliefs. More than anything his energy helps us overcome any negative chatter going on in our minds. JP is a leader in the area of how to master your life, how to own your life, how to live a life of no regrets. In his book 'How to Own Your Life' he will teach you how to live the life that you will want to talk about, and how to make your life a bestselling story!

Love always,

Lisa Nichols.

Foreword Lisa Nichols

Foreword Daniel Priestley

A few trips around the sun. That's all we get.

JEAN-PIERRE DE VILLIERS

I f all goes well, we get about 80-90 trips around the sun. If you're lucky you'll get 100 laps; many people are given a lot less. Each of us really doesn't know how many more trips around the sun we have left.

The first 10 trips around the sun we hardly remember. The last 10 we spend mostly reminiscing. A third of our lives we are asleep, a lot of our time is spent doing the stuff we have to do - eating, commuting or checking Facebook.

We get barely a moment in time that is "our life".

Many people worry about making the most of their time here. We worry about sucking the juice of each day or making a big enough impact to leave a positive legacy.

There are two great mistakes a person can make in life. Firstly, you could just drift through life never asking tough questions or taking bold actions. Secondly, succumbing to the expectations and pressures of others rather than living the life you truly want to live.

Making brave decisions and acting accordingly is what JP calls "owning your life".

It's about finding the balance that works for you. Filling up your days with things that matter to you and hopefully making a positive difference to others.

Is it possible to take greater ownership over your life? Are you in the driver's seat? Are you in control or are you at the whims of fate?

In this book, JP proves that you are in control of a lot more than you think. He takes a radical approach - you are responsible for all of it, you are in control of your reality, your destiny and you can radically steer the direction of your life wherever you choose. For better or worse, you have to "own it" though, if you ever hope to get to a place of satisfaction with life.

It's easy to get complacent. We all have a comfort zone and by definition we like it there. This book is a bittersweet gift from JP to nudge us out of the safe little bubble we're in and into the life we know we're capable of.

JP is good at this, he's honed his skills on some difficult cases. He regularly takes CEOs, athletes and celebrities out of their comfort zones and into better, more meaningful lives. These high-achieving people aren't easy to work with. They have enviable lives, and by most people's standards, they don't need more motivation. JP has a talent for finding a way to challenge, stress test and empower people of all walks of life into new heights.

He knows that each of them has more to give and more to get from life. Each of us has the power to impact the world positively.

Although we do not know the scale of the impact we will have, each of us must make our best effort to make the most of our time. Each of us must strike a balance between serving others or savouring life ourselves - enjoying a sensuous lifestyle and creating an impact in the lives of others.

I believe that no one ever gets to know their legacy. No one can plan it, no one can orchestrate it, and no one can claim theirs is better or more impactful than anyone else.

Vincent Van Gogh went to his grave believing he was nothing more than a madman and a failed artist. He will never know that his gallery in Amsterdam is one of the most visited in the world or that his art hangs in the National Gallery alongside Leonardo DaVinci.

Dr Erasmus Darwin was a great inventor, doctor and humanitarian. He would have believed that his greatest achievements were his own and would never have known that his grandson, Charles, would advance his basic theories around the idea of evolution and write a book that would change the way we see ourselves as a species.

The mother and father of Marie Curie made enormous sacrifices so that their daughter might go to university. They would never know that she would win two Nobel Prizes for her work in physics and chemistry and impact billions of lives. If you asked them whether all the hard work and sacrifice was worth it, they may have harboured their doubts.

I believe that every person plays an important role on this planet and that all success must be viewed in a broader context rather than in isolation.

If humanity is a rich tapestry, some people are on show and are an obvious feature on that tapestry, however, their very existence depends on every other thread that is weaving the masterpiece in place.

I know in my life there are people who influenced me greatly who have no idea just how much they did. I also know that many of them are not known or famous in any way, some of them don't even know who I am, but I was influenced by their books or their talks.

Sometimes being a good friend, sending a thoughtful letter, showing compassion to a stranger or sharing an authentic moment can spark a chain of events that impacts the world.

Who knows what impact you will have if you really take ownership of your life.

Foreword Daniel Priestley

"

YOU HAVE TO GET OUT OF YOUR OWN WAY.

Prologue

If I could sum up my daily approach to life in one sentence it would be this: I do whatever it takes to be better. Everything I do, in every aspect of my life, is about not simply settling for 'good' but striving for 'better'. I want to be a better leader to the people and world that I love. I want to be a better husband to my amazing wife, a better brother to my cherished siblings and a better son to my inspirational mother. I want to do better at supporting my friends through whatever they're experiencing, good or bad, and at being a diligent student to my mentors and coaches. I always want to do my very best for this planet and all its inhabitants. Why? Because I and everyone and everything in my life deserve that much from me.

Growing up in South Africa may have made his achievements much more real and personal for me but wherever I'd been born, I'm certain that Nelson Mandela would still have been my hero. How could you not admire that man?

He spent 27 years locked up in the harshest of prison environments for trying to do better for his people. 27 years. It's long enough to kick the fire out of most people and yet when he was eventually released, his absolute passion to do better burned as brightly as it ever had. He went on to lead an entire nation, stood up for the poor and those dealing with HIV and won a Nobel Peace Prize among many, many other awards. A truly astonishing example to us all.

As I strive to make my own improvements day-by-day, I often hear Mandela's famous quotation ringing in my ears: "There is no passion to be found living a life that is less than the one you are capable of living." Wow. There's so much motivation in that sentence. For a start, who wants to live a life free from passion? That would seem a very empty existence indeed. Securing that passion requires us to live the life we're "capable of living." Think about that.

What Mandela is saying is that regardless of where you are in your life right now, you should never tell yourself that you've done enough. Or, at the other end of the spectrum, if things aren't going so well for you and life feels like it's dragging you down, then you should never give up, never quit, if you want to get that passion back. What an inspiring sentiment.

If you like your soundbites even shorter then you could distil that thought down to the two words in one of my favourite questions: what if? What if! I love that question. If you approach life with that question at the front of your mind, then who knows what you might achieve. What if you could be a little bit fitter? What if your business did a little bit better? What if you could be a little bit happier? It's the start of so many wonderful possibilities.

That spirit of 'what if?' is exactly why I make a constant effort to be a brilliant student of life. I am brilliant in my growth and brilliant in seeking my genius. Note that I wrote 'brilliant', not 'perfect'. I am a long way from perfect and make no claim upon it; which is why I'm also brilliant in my imperfections and in my failures. Because sometimes, perhaps even often, I'll fall short of where I want to be. That's OK. I'm very much cool with that.

And you should be too. Because we're all brilliant, shining lights and we all have the capacity to shine more brightly if we'd only ask, "what if?" If we'd only try to live the life we're capable of living. Don't spend time fixating on your imperfections today or exaggerating yesterday's successes. Tomorrow is a new day and you can either rest on your laurels, settle for what you have now, or you can own your life, strive for that passion and aim to be better every minute of every day. This isn't something available only to me or to a select few, it's achievable by everyone as of this very minute – you included.

But first, before you can truthfully say

you're doing the best you can and are able to give yourself the opportunity to attain the most from life, you have to give yourself permission. You have to get out of your own way.

"

DO NOT FEAR
FAILURE; MAKE
FRIENDS WITH IT.

Embrace failure

JEAN-PIERRE DE VILLIERS

Y ou, me, every single one of us can be better. That's an unshakeable belief I hold that's so central to me, it feels like part of my genetic coding, my DNA. It's what gets me up in the morning, knowing that every day I'll try my absolute best to do whatever it takes to improve. It's a drive which means that with every new sunrise, I'm unflinchingly certain that no matter how good I was yesterday or the day before, I can still be better than I was then and better than I am now.

Exactly the same goes for you – if you give yourself the chance.

I've already talked about Nelson Mandela's journey and demonstrated that this innate capability to improve is as much within any great leader you can think of as it is you. Whoever you and wherever you feel you are in life, no matter what you've achieved, if you start to think you've done it all, to tell yourself that you're the best, that you're the number one, then that's the day you start to falter and fall. We're all part of nature and nothing in nature ever stays the same. If you're the sort of person that puts your own achievements on a pedestal, then it's time for you to tear that pedestal down and see yourself for the human being you are. You must realise that, as part of nature, you need to evolve to keep pace. You have not reached your finish line.

Life is triumph and tragedy and I can tell you from first-hand experience that positive change comes not only from breakthroughs but from breakdowns. This is an important lesson. We must embrace both the light and the shade. So, as you continue your personal journey for betterment, ask yourself not only, "what am I running towards?" but, "what am I running from?" If you've turned away from something in the hope that you can block it out and avoid its influence or its consequences, then I'm here to tell you that it's only a matter of time before you come screeching to a halt and that dark shadow catches up with you and forces you to confront it. It is your job not to avoid this confrontation but to turn and face those difficulties you know about as early as you can and on your own terms. Put yourself in control of that interaction and if that means failure, well, then embrace that failure.

If you haven't worked it out yet or have been skirting around the subject trying to avoid its true reality, then let me spell it out for you: you are going to fail. Again, and again and again. But don't worry, I have a wish for you – although not the one you're expecting. My wish for you is that failure comes knocking at your door very loudly and with great urgency. It might not sound like it to you at first, but this wish is born out of my love for you. Because failure is such a beautiful life lesson.

Here's a bit of virtual role play. Imagine you're the owner of a business. Everything your business touches turns to gold and you can't put a foot wrong. You've got no competitors, no challenge and you're at the top of the tree, lapping it all up. Sounds great, right? Of course, it does. At first. But keep imagining this scenario as it carries on for year after year after year. You and your business just coasting along, doing the same old thing from sunrise to sunset every day. Forever. You've got no reason to change or to try anything new, you just sit at that big wooden desk on the top floor of your office, staring at the clock, waiting to go home again. You're B-O-R-E-D. Your heart is crying out for some form of challenge. Anything that feels like a kind of risk or adventure which will make you work a little bit harder and dig a little bit deeper. There is so much reward to be gained from failure and the threat of failure and your heart will thank you for the exposure to it.

That's if you've got out of your own way. If you haven't, then your head is still in control. Your head doesn't want any of that challenge or jeopardy stuff. Its sole objective is to help you survive. It doesn't care about what you want inside, about your need for nourishment and fulfilment. It just wants you to live. Now sometimes this is incredibly helpful. If you're confronted by a bear in the woods that looks like it wants to eat you for lunch, then I strongly suggest you follow your head's instinct for survival. But these days, most of us don't spend that much time squaring up to hungry bears. Your mind simply wants you to think that the peril you're experiencing, by which I mean your potential for failure, is on that sort of scale when the reality is far less dangerous and more enriching. Ignore the persistent voice that tells you you're no good and never will be any good so don't even bother trying, because that's the sound of your head getting in the way of your heart. Do not fear failure; make friends with it.

"

IT'S YOUR STORY
AND YOU HAVE THE
POWER TO
CHANGE IT.

Change your story

JEAN-PIERRE DE VILLIERS

L earning to embrace failure is a critical step on the path to getting out of your own way. If I was coaching you through your journey, there would be two more things I'd tell you from the outset to get you pointing in the right direction. Firstly, I don't care where you are right now, I care about where you're headed tomorrow and secondly, I don't care what you think about me, I only care what you think about you. Consider those ideas for a moment and how they relate to you. For me, I think of them as pre-conditions that frame my constant endeavour to be better.

So where do you want to be going tomorrow? What is that superhuman, blue sky version of yourself that you want to aim for? If you could wave a magic wand over yourself and your life, whisper a secret spell and become anything at all, what and where would you choose to be? Is your dream to be exactly where you're sat or stood at this very second, reading these words on this page to yourself? I bet it isn't. I bet your dream looks nothing like this particular moment. Which of course begs one very obvious follow-up question: why are you not there right now?

Because you're getting in your own way! It's your fault.

OK, let's take a brief reality check. You may be sitting there right now saying, "Oh really, JP? Well, my dream is to be an astronaut, but I flunked maths at school so I'm hardly in a position to submit my CV to NASA right now, am I? What do you say to that, eh?"

Fine, that's fair enough, I totally respect the need for you to introduce cold, hard, realistic limitations based on your prior knowledge. But where are you now? Are you sat at one of two hundred desks in a school sports hall, silently flunking your maths exams? No! I'm not telling you that you can just go out and be whatever you want. I'm saying that you can do anything you want if you give yourself permission and step out of your own way. You have to make that leap. Staying where you are, repeating, "I can't, I can't, I can't" will not work for you. It's time for you to change your tune! Nothing is ever in the way, everything is always on the way.

If you're in one place and you spend your whole life daydreaming about being in some other place, then it's only you who is stopping yourself from heading there now. Your life is determined by your actions. It's your story and you have the power to change it.

"

IT'S ABOUT GIVING
YOU THE BEST
CHANCE POSSIBLE
TO BE A BETTER
VERSION OF YOU
EVERY SINGLE DAY.

Set the standards

JEAN-PIERRE DE VILLIERS

I make the point about being in control of your own story for a couple of reasons. As I made clear in the previous section, only you can be the architect of your own future. But there's an important flip side to the meaning of that realisation – if only you can change you, then you have neither the right nor the power to change anyone else.

It's something that comes up a lot in my coaching work. I hear people say things like, "Oh, if only I could get him or her to do or see things differently then everything would be so much better." People who think like this are focusing on the wrong problem – one they can't resolve and one which will lead them to frustration and despair if they continue to pursue it. You must understand that you cannot control anyone, whether it's friends, family, lovers or your apparent enemies.

Armed with this awareness, if you sense irreconcilable difficulties in aspects of your relationships with people, or if you're uncomfortable about the limitations you feel they place on you, there are two, stark choices available: either change how you interact with them or stop being around them altogether.

That latter option is tough. Nobody wants to throw people out of their lives on a whim but sometimes it's the only appropriate course of action. Remember, you're trying to get out of your own way – your first responsibility is to look after yourself – and when you surround yourself exclusively with the right people, I guarantee that you'll find yourself heading in the right direction. In most cases, however, you'll want to try to change your interactions first and a great way to do this is by setting boundaries, or standards as I refer to them.

It's your life, so it's perfectly legitimate for you to set non-negotiable standards around specific behaviours or traits. But you need to be clear with yourself and able to clearly articulate what you need, otherwise your plan is doomed to failure from the outset. (Of course, if your plan does fail, don't forget to embrace the failure too.)

You might choose to set standards based on trust, authenticity, gratitude, honesty or a particular set of beliefs. Whatever you choose, it's essential that, once you've spelt them out to yourself and everyone they affect, that you maintain them at all costs. This is not a case of simply holding other people to account. There's no room for double standards here; you must also judge yourself by the strict standards that you hold so dear.

The standards that you set reflect the quality of your life and that should be clear for all to see the moment that you step into a room. We all understand that not only do first impressions count, they also last. For better or for worse, it can be hard for people to shake the perception they form of you in those first, crucial seconds and minutes that you meet. So, you'd better make damn sure that you set the right tone. Consider everything – your physical shape, your posture, your clothing, your attitude, your hygiene, your happiness… It's all on display, whether you like it or not. Be 100% certain that the standards you set match your own reality and form part of your daily rituals and habits. There's no sense in setting tough standards if you don't put regular effort in to practising and living up to them.

Re-read that last sentence because it's critical to your success here. Don't forget, we're talking about getting to where you want to be. About a process of constant self-improvement. There's no point whatsoever setting standards that reflect where you are now. Your standards should be pointing you at your destination and helping you achieve your goals. That's why you need to constantly contribute effort to maintain and work towards them. It's about giving you the best chance possible to be a better version of you every single day.

Set the standards

"

THAT'S ALL UP TO
YOU, BUT YOU HAVE
TO START TODAY.

Start today

JEAN-PIERRE DE VILLIERS

When I talk about being better tomorrow, I don't mean that feeling you might get when you know a difficult task is hanging over you. I don't mean, "I'll do that tomorrow." That's just an excuse. It's a delaying tactic by your head to ensure you stay right where you are, without challenging yourself. Do not fall into that trap.

I'm not telling you this because I smugly think that I've got my entire life all figured out and perfect. I haven't. But I promise you that I'm constantly working at figuring it out and constantly growing and striving with every out breath I take. That was true yesterday, it's true today and it will be true tomorrow as well. There is no moment like this moment – so grab it, and start getting better NOW.

Ask yourself a question: are you a different, better person to the one you were a month ago? Be honest with yourself. If the answer is no, that you haven't changed in a whole 30 days, then what are doing?! You only get 12 of these bad boys a year, don't waste any of them! Every ticking second counts.

Change might come about for a whole variety of reasons – failure, fulfilment or success, to name but three. The key is whether you can say you've played an active part in shaping that change within yourself. Don't convince yourself that you're not ready and instead need to wait for one of many possible delaying tactics – like a good night's sleep or some decisive future event to take place – get on with it immediately. That's what your heart wants you to do. Procrastination is what your head wants you to do.

It's not as if I or anyone else is asking you to be perfect every day from this moment onwards. I don't expect you to revolutionise your life in just one day and neither should you. In fact, I don't even expect you to be your best every day. Instead, I think you should do your best every day. It's a subtle difference but a truly important one. And if you don't do your best every day? Here comes the tough love: I think you're selfish.

Selfish because the most amazing thing you can do in life is give. The great Tony Robbins sums it up best when he says, "The secret to living is giving." Whether it's physically, emotionally, psychologically or spiritually, if you're not showing up, aiming to be the very best version of yourself from morning until night and back to morning again, you're sabotaging yourself and you're sabotaging all those people you surround yourself with who love you and rely on you. You're getting in your own way.

I once had a client who had been overweight their whole life. I'm telling you this story with love. I do my very best not to judge anyone for anything and as I said before, I don't care what you think about me, I only care what you think about you. In this case, my client was overweight and clearly unhappy about it. I don't just mean they'd put on a few pounds, I mean they were heavily overweight. It was an intolerably heavy physical and emotional load for this person to carry.

But this client was telling themselves tale after tale about the past and present and setting barrier after barrier for the future. There was a whole host of reasons why nothing had ever changed and all of them came from the head's desire to stay safe in its comfort zone. The heart wasn't getting a look in. So, I put myself in this person's shoes and told them honestly what I thought. I said, "If I was your weight and felt like you do about it, I would wake up and realise that I should run 24 hours a day until I lost both the physical and emotional weight." And that's all it took. I told them the truth from my perspective, the lightbulb went off in that person's head and they're now a much happier, healthier and fitter human being.

Do you see what I was really saying? I

was saying, "You are in your own way. Wake up! No one is coming to save you. There is no rescue party on the lookout for you. Get out of your own way and change your story." That's not to say that anyone has to do everything on their own. In fact, the result of giving yourself permission in this way may be to finally ask a person for that help you've always wanted but have been too afraid to seek. It's a great idea to involve other people in your progress – it aids your motivation and they may help to hold you accountable. That's all up to you, but you have to start today.

"

TRUST ME, YOU'RE GOING TO FEEL MUCH BETTER.

Get moving

JEAN-PIERRE DE VILLIERS

I t's no accident that I chose to tell you a story about someone who lost a lot of weight as a great example of a person finally getting out of their own way once the light was switched on for them. I know for certain that good exercise and maintaining excellent fitness are central to your ability to do your best every day.

I described the impact of standards earlier and fitness is a non-negotiable standard I set for myself and others. I wonder if you considered it as a potential standard when you read that chapter? Chances are that you didn't – most people seem not to. Instead, they come up with notions like gratitude or trust. Why? Because it feels so much easier to say you're going to be trustworthy. It doesn't involve you hitting the gym, lifting weights, doing burpees or fitting a 10-mile run into your daily routine. It doesn't require you to take a big action or make a big commitment. Instead of shirking them, I urge you to face up to those big commitments, especially when it comes to fitness, because doing so will help you deliver all those other mental attributes like trust and integrity that you're striving for.

I've yet to meet a single person in my life who's gone for a workout, a run, a swim or any kind of effortful aerobic exercise and then come out of the gym to say, "Oh, I just finished my workout. I feel so… depressed." No one ever says that! The opposite is always true. The scientists will tell you that the process of exercising creates all kinds of wonderful activity in your body that leaves you feeling more positive than you were before you started. It's a fact!

Organisations helping people with depression encourage those individuals to get moving if they want to improve their mental state. If you're reading this and you're feeling down, then I echo those words. Get out there and move your ass! It doesn't have to cost you a thing, it takes far less time than you think –

less time than you'll spend sitting there trying to miserably justify all the reasons why you shouldn't do it – and it feels extraordinary. Moving your body, satisfying your heart and firing up your mind is beautiful and makes you feel connected and incredible. If you do nothing else, making that one effort to boost your fitness will make you a happier, more well-rounded person.

If you choose to avoid fitness and don't engage with trying to lead a more active lifestyle then you're seriously compromising your capability to achieve what you want, full stop. You're at the other end of the spectrum. Maybe you're already a super-fit beast who understands the virtue of putting in the work. That's great. But don't for one second sit back and think you've checked the box or 'done' that. How can you get better? What can you do today that you didn't do yesterday? Are you still trying to be fitter or are you coasting along, stuck in your safe, current reality? Wherever you are on the scale, there's always room to grow.

Everyone wants to be inspired and the greatest way to inspire is to live an inspirational life. Should you need some inspiration then come and follow me online and you'll see that I practise what I preach. That way, you won't need to just read my words, you can watch and hear the sound of my feet as they pound the pavement every day when I run. I am totally out of my own way and whether it's boxing, cycling, Ironman triathlon or anything else, I keep working hard at my fitness knowing that I can keep on growing.

Just like I said in the last chapter, you need to start today. And you need to not only set out with good intentions, you need to also keep those intentions alive through whatever comes your way. If it's snowing out and you can't open your front door, that's no excuse to slouch back down on the sofa with a chocolate bar and give up. Find another way to get the exercise you need. You could be doing yoga, jumping, burpees, shadow boxing, Pilates... even having some good sex! There's always an alternative option, including during those times when you're tired, injured or in a different part of the world that you don't know. However, you choose to get your daily activity, as the slogan goes, just do it. Trust me, you're going to feel much better.

"

WHEN YOU'RE
ACTIVE AND YOU
LEAVE YOUR EGO
BEHIND, YOU LET
YOUR HEART IN AND
YOU START ACTING
WITH PASSION.

"

Prove your passion

JEAN-PIERRE DE VILLIERS

In a moment, I'm going to ask you to demonstrate your commitment to your own genuine desire for improvement. It'll only take a few seconds, but your engagement with it will tell me, and you, everything we need to know about your determination. We'll find out whether you're reading this because you really, truly want to get out of your way or whether you're just a tourist, here for the nice view. It'll only take 10 seconds of your life. What were you going to do with those 10 seconds otherwise, I wonder?

I want to show you what getting out of your own way feels like. What giving yourself permission to feel alive looks and feels like. I'm going to ask you to stop reading, just for ten seconds, and to celebrate as loudly and passionately as you're able. Give it everything.

I don't care where you are right now or about any other aspect of your situation or context. "I would, but…" is not a valid option. Prove to yourself that you're serious about owning your life and getting out of your own way. If you're currently sitting there squirming and thinking of excuses you can comfort yourself with about how to avoid doing this then, I'm sorry to be so direct, you're one of the people who needs to engage with this exercise the most. You're stuck. If you can't even get out of your own way while reading a book about getting out of your own way, what chance do you have of making significant improvements to your attitude and your life? You might want to spend some time reflecting on why that might be.

So, when I prompt you shortly, just do this one thing with me. Go for it with everything you've got and have fun with it. Be playful. What do you have to lose that's of any real significance? It's a mere 10 seconds, that's all.

In the last chapter, I highlighted the intense importance of fitness and exercise in your life. As should have become clear to you by now, my insistence on making the effort to get active isn't simply about adding a few more years to your life, it's about injecting more vitality, energy, positivity, enthusiasm and passion into your existence. Otherwise, what's the point of it all? Do you really want to live for a hundred years of just feeling like you're enduring it all, day-by-day? Life doesn't have to be – shouldn't be – like that.

For me, passion is one of the greatest ingredients in the world. If you want an amazing relationship, add some passion. If you want a successful business, add some passion. If you want to surround yourself with a happy environment, add some passion. Passion proves you're committed and that you care. That's why I'm asking you to show just 10 seconds of your genuine passion.

Why 10 seconds? Because it's just the right length of time for you to prove that you're prepared to make a change. It's just on the far side of your comfort levels. For the first second or two, you'll feel completely fine about what you're doing. In fact, you'll barely even notice you're doing anything until after you've done it. When you reach three to five seconds your brain is likely to start kicking in and you'll begin thinking about what it is that you're doing. Everything else that's going on around you will get sucked into your thoughts too. You'll become very aware of yourself and question what's happening: "Am I doing too much or too little? Are other people staring at or listening to me? Do I look or sound like an idiot? What's going to happen when I finish?" In other words, your ego is going to show up and it's not going to like what it sees. I want you to smash right through that. To pull out another five seconds of unbridled celebration in the face of your uncertainty. Square up to your ego and send it packing.

Maybe you also want some motivation. Perhaps you're questioning why you should be celebrating at all. The answer's simple: because you can! You're breathing, you're alive, you're here. The sky is above, and the ground is below.

What more motivation do you need?

OK then, are you ready? Here goes.

Three, two, one, CELEBRATE!!!

Welcome back. So how did it go? How do you feel? Quickly check in with yourself and report back on your immediate emotions and sensations. I do this same exercise at some of the events I speak at. We're talking big rooms stuffed full of people all sitting politely, side-by-side. When I suggest this to them you can sense the atmosphere in the room shifting. There's usually an outbreak of nervous laughter. And then they do it, all celebrating like a football crowd who's just watched their team win the World Cup. Ten seconds of total chaos and nobody outside that room has a clue what's going on. As soon as we stop, there's an incredible, obvious energy in the room. Everyone smiling, laughing and suddenly desperate to talk to the person next to them that they've been studiously ignoring until that point a short while ago when, five seconds into their celebrating, both people started wondering whether they looked better or worse than the other person did.

I ask people to give themselves a round of applause, so feel free to do the same for yourself if you got stuck in. Then, once I've managed to settle everyone down – for the room is now packed full of electricity and positive vibes – I ask them how they feel. I noted down the responses I heard from them last time I did this: "Amazing… stunning… fantastic… full of life… refreshed… powerful…" Do you feel the same way? Isn't it incredible that just letting go for 10 seconds can make you feel like this? I think this is how you should always feel. So why don't you? Because you don't give yourself permission to do so. Because your head, with its range of fears and limiting beliefs, is in control and barking at you all the time. When you're active and you leave your ego behind, you let your heart in and you start acting with passion.

"

YOU CAN LOCK ON TO THE BEST TARGETS WITH CERTAINTY AND GIVE THEM EVERYTHING YOU'VE GOT, WITHOUT ANY REGRETS.

"

Trust your intuition

JEAN-PIERRE DE VILLIERS

L earning to trust your intuition is an extremely powerful and profound change that you can make to your life. It's not necessarily something you can just switch on immediately with a click of the fingers. But with practice, by paying more attention to the idea of intuition and pausing to understand what you might intuit rather than simply accepting the seemingly rational response your mind provides, you can re-wire yourself to take advantage of the opportunities it creates.

Growth, contribution, spirituality, faith, intuition. For me, these are all spiritual, heart-centric ways of living that make you feel good and drive you to act in a positive manner. Trusting your intuition will lead you to start making decisions stemming from what feels good, which is something I wholeheartedly recommend. It will encourage you to do your best – don't forget, I'm making that subtle distinction between doing your best and being the best and you and everyone around you will appreciate that continual effort as it begins to feel increasingly natural to you. I also reiterate that if you go out there trying to be the best, there's a very high probability that life will come and punch you in the face real soon. If that happens to you, take the beautiful lesson, learn from it and move on.

Your intuition is a representation of what's going on in your heart, whereas your constant attempts at rationalisation are all led by your head. I'm going to keep pushing this point because changing your perspective on your own decision-making process is so important to your ongoing transformation, but it takes effort and practice to achieve. You'll need to keep reminding yourself to do it at first before it comes naturally to you. This is another form of exercise, mental this time rather than physical, for you to get your teeth into and work at. Don't be disheartened if at first you don't think you're acting intuitively enough. Keep reminding yourself and focus on listening to your heart and it will eventually all fall into place.

One of the genuinely fantastic benefits of learning to use your intuition more is that you're getting outstanding advice from a wise and experienced person (that's you) for free. In trying to look for solutions to your problems, you're liable to look in many different places for answers. Unfortunately, when you're desperate, not all of the sources you attempt to rely upon are reliable. Whereas if you go with your heart and put everything into the course of action it's leading you towards, you'll more frequently find yourself on the path that's right for you.

So much can be achieved by seeking guidance inwardly instead of outwardly. Improve your body and soul through daily fitness, through meditation, through breathing and even through hydrating properly. All of these things can help you become happier and more fulfilled because they lead you to feel right from the inside instead of judging yourself against others and seeking guidance from people who don't know you anywhere near as well as you know yourself. It all goes back to controlling what you can control, which is you and your life, not the lives of others.

By the way, since I mention hydration, I wanted to add that a frighteningly high number of people don't get enough water into their bodies, despite the fact that it's scientifically proven that staying well hydrated improves cognition and focus. If you're not currently getting enough water – and I do mean water, not flat whites, cappuccinos, lattes or, worse still, alcohol – then changing your daily drinking habits is another quick, easy and free win for you. Keep a water bottle with you at all times!

As you learn to trust your intuition more and more, I strongly recommend that you develop a moral framework, that you can articulate to yourself, around which to hang your decision-making. This is the concept of values. Most people have a set of values but, often, they haven't really thought about them very much. It's a smart idea to bring these into sharper focus because they will guide your intuition in the right direction for your individual personality. We are all unique with different outlooks and compasses inside of us. Make sure you truly understand where your compass is pointing. If you're unsure about the idea of values, then I seriously suggest you look up the work of Dr. John Demartini. He's a living legend in the field and a truly inspirational guy. His advice works, so take it.

Once you know what your values are then your intuition will laser-guide you towards the opportunities that are best for you – and steer you away from those ones that might turn out to be too good to be true. You can lock on to the best targets with certainty and give them everything you've got, without any regrets.

"

IT'S NOT ROCKET
SCIENCE,
IT'S PUTTING IN
THE EFFORT.

"

Live regret-free

JEAN-PIERRE DE VILLIERS

"You can't take it with you." That's how the saying usually goes. The inference is that there's no point in hoarding material possessions or wasting time on your business because the only things you're going to be buried with are your regrets. Well, let me make one thing very plain: I have precisely zero intention of dying with any regrets. And neither should you.

What are regrets apart from clear evidence that there were moments in your life when you didn't get out of your own way to do what your heart told you should be doing? Regrets are the product of not doing everything that it takes to own your life. Nobody wants to have regrets – I think we can agree that they're a 100% negative feature of life and have no upsides – and that's why I urge you to do whatever it takes to be the best version of yourself.

That simple act comes with an enormous benefit. Because if you do whatever it takes in life then, even if you fail, you won't label yourself as a failure. You did your best. You gave it everything. Good effort. It's an approach which draws admiration, praise and respect. As soon as you let shame or regret into your life, it indicates that you didn't do your best somewhere along the line. And let me reassure you once again that I'm encouraging you to attempt your best; I'm not demanding that you try to be perfect.

Here's a personal example. I recently completed the world's toughest full-distance Ironman triathlon. It was incredibly hard, but I did it; well inside the time I'd hoped to beat. When I was a teenage boy, a doctor told my mum and I that I'd never be able to run again. Ever since that day, I've done my best to prove him wrong. When I was training for the Ironman, I didn't know how it would turn out, but I was determined to put everything into it. With the mental and physical approach that I took, it wouldn't have been a problem if I'd spent months gearing up for the big day and then failed to finish. There would have been no shame and I wouldn't have regretted a thing about it because I'd have known that I'd always done my best.

I take exactly the same principle into the rest of my life. If a relationship, a business, a journey or anything else doesn't pan out then I haven't lost anything because I'm still proud of the way I tackled it. This 'no regrets' mentality gives me an extra layer of armour-plating. Don't worry about me, I'll always be OK. I should also add that once you start acting like this, the chances of anything you do not working out become greatly reduced. It's a real win-win approach – if you put in the effort.

Effort is vitally important. You can't expect any of this to conveniently fall into your lap. Yes, you might get lucky – but you probably won't. It's all well and good to read inspirational books and turn up at motivational events as long as you realise that the real work starts when you put the book down or when you walk out of the auditorium.

Tony Robbins calls it a repetition – that time when you have to take the learning you've been given and turn it into something repeatable that forms part of your routine, out in the wild of your daily life. You need to do it again and again, with conscious practice, until it becomes a part of the fabric of your being. It's not something you can just do for a week, a month or even a year. You have to keep making the effort to be your best forever. As you experience and drive change throughout your life, you need to raise your standards, make better decisions, take control of your own fitness and listen to your own heart over and above the opinions of others. You must go out into the world and practice, succeed and fail time and time again. Everything in this book is the non-negotiable core of getting out of your own way. It is how you will make progress – sometimes steadily and almost imperceptibly, other times in giant, revelatory leaps. It's not rocket science, it's putting in the effort.

"

BE THE BEST YOU
CAN BE, EVERY
DAY, AND REAP
THE REWARDS YOU
ALWAYS THOUGHT
WERE OUT OF YOUR
REACH.

Make it your fault

Jean-Pierre De Villiers

Earlier on in this book, I wrote that I don't care what you think about me, I only care what you think about you. The reason that I don't care what you think about me is that I'm already unshakeable in my belief that I'm out of my own way. That wasn't always the case. As a younger man, I lived a life where I was constantly getting in my own way. But once I woke up and realised that everything needed to change, I went from being own worst enemy to my own best friend. I don't need to care what others think about me anymore and, in time, neither will you.

The last part of this chapter's opening sentence, 'I only care what you think about you' is just as sincerely felt. We may have never met, but I care about you and I want the very best for you. In order for you to realise that potential, though, you must recognise that, from this moment on, you're responsible for everything. You've read the truths contained in this book so there are no excuses available any more – your life is your responsibility. No 'ifs', no 'buts'. It's time for you to step up.

If you're unhappy with any aspect of your life, are striving to make a success out of something or have just realised that there's more to existence then the daily grind you're putting yourself through, there's a quote that you may already know which sums up my response to your situation: "If you don't like where you are, move! You're not a tree." That sentiment applies as much to mental states and life fulfilment as it does to geography and place. It puts the burden of responsibility squarely onto your shoulders. Not the government, not your boss, not your partner; you.

If you feel you're stuck in a dead-end job that you hate, with no chance of escape, then it's your fault. If you find yourself in a relationship that once used to provide so much joy, but which has since deteriorated from thriving to surviving to suffering, then it's your fault. If you're sitting on your couch getting drunk because your business dream is going nowhere, it's your fault.

Maybe you're thinking, "Hang on a minute JP, that might be a touch harsh. It can't all be my fault." Yet the moment you start opening your heart to thoughts like that is the moment that you give away all of your power. Please, don't do that. If you've read through the whole of this book, and especially if you made the effort to take part in the celebration exercise earlier, then you've come so far already. Don't throw away what you've gained. Understand that by framing everything as your own fault, you have total control of your life and the ultimate freedom to change.

So please, if you really want to own your life and you respect what you've just read, do me a favour. Do yourself an even bigger favour. Whatever success or fulfilment looks and feels like to you, the moment this paragraph ends, resolve to spend the rest of your life doing whatever it takes to get out of your own way. Not just for you, not just for me, but for everyone in your life and in the world around you. Be the best you can be, every day, and reap the rewards you always thought were out of your reach.

Make it your fault

About The Author

JEAN-PIERRE DE VILLIERS

Jean-Pierre, or JP as he is known, is the world's leading CEO Coach. JP coaches his clients how to perform at their best, so they have more energy, focus and better results.

JP has two decades of experience in personal coaching and high performance; he also runs events, retreats and challenges around the world.

He has worked with CEO's, Celebrities, Olympic athletes and other influential men and women who demand the best from themselves and in their lives including Olympic gold medalists, Actors and Award-winning film Directors and Producers.

Jean-Pierre's clients maximise their potential and get the most out of their life. JP teaches them the strategies to build and maintain a high-performance body and mind.

As well as speaking internationally, Jean-

Pierre regularly contributes to publications and features in the media. He is the author of several books and was voted as Health Coach of the year. JP was selected as one of the most inspiring people in London and has had the honour of speaking in front of the Royal family in the UAE.

JP has featured as an international trainer for Success Resources, the No.1 educational events company in the world, the leading seminar organiser in the U.A.E. Najahi Events, and as a representative for the No.1 Success Coach in the world, Tony Robbins.

"I am in the energy, health and wealth management business and have been delivering high-performance results for two decades. What I teach is based on what works at the highest end of the market, having worked with the best of the best. I am fully committed to powerfully improving the quality of your life."

About The Author

HOW
TO
OWN
YOUR
LIFE

Get out of your own way and
live your life with no regrets.

FIRST EDITION

JEAN-PIERRE DE VILLIERS

About The Author

36735153R00078

Printed in Poland
by Amazon Fulfillment
Poland Sp. z o.o., Wrocław